Alif
to
Yaa

Zarir Muhammad

A Student of the Hifzul Quran
Islamic Academy, Windsor, ON
Canada

Editor

Abeer Elsayed

Al-Quranul Karim Teacher,
Rose City Islamic Center (RCIC),
Windsor, ON, Canada

ا - اَللّٰهُ

Alif is for Allah (SWT).

Allah created humans and everything around us.

Allah (SWT) controls the whole Universe.

Baa is for Bismillah.

**Bismillah means
"In the name of Allah (SWT)."**

**We say Bismillah before starting
every activity.**

ت - تَقْوٰى

Taa is for Taqwa.

Taqwa means fear of Allah (SWT).

Taqwa guides us in being good humans, as all our good or evil activities are noted by Allah (SWT) and will be rewarded or punished accordingly.

ث - ثَوَابٌ

Thaa is for Thawab.

Thawab means the reward of Allah (SWT).

Doing good deeds can increase our thawab.

Jeem is for Jannah.

Jannah means paradise.

If we believe in Allah (SWT), we will go to Jannah.

Ha is for Hajj.

Hajj is a pilgrimage that Muslims try to make at least once in their lifetime.

**When we go for Hajj,
we can see the houses of Allah (SWT)
and the Prophet Muhammad (SAW).**

Kha is for Khairun.

Khairun means the best.

**The lifestyle of
the Prophet Muhammad (SAW)
is the best for us to follow.**

د - دَعْوَةٌ

Daal is for Dawah.

Dawah is an invitation to people to embrace Islam.

We practice and give dawah to promote the truth.

ذ - ذِكْرٌ

Zhaal is for Zikr.

Zikr means remembrance of Allah (SWT).

We have to carry the name of Allah (SWT) in our minds and hearts all the time.

Raa is for Ramadan.

Ramadan is a time when we fast.

We fast for 30 days during Ramadan.

ز - زَكوٰةٌ

Zaa is for Zakat.

Zakat is a pillar of Islam.

People have to give zakat during Ramadan.

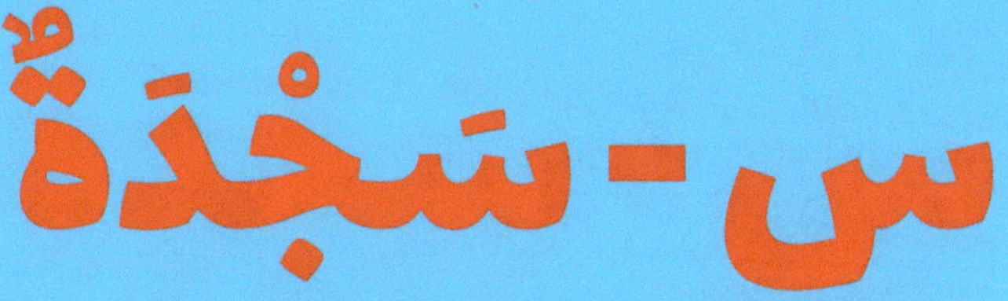

س - سَجْدَةٌ

Seen is for Sajdah.

Sajdah is a Muslim prayer.

We perform sajdahs five times a day.

ش - شِرْكٌ

Sheen is for Sharik.

Sharik means to think
that Allah (SWT) has partners.
It is a great sin.

Allah acts alone. Allah has no wife,
children, or partners like humans have.

ص - صَبْرٌ

Saad is for Sabrun.

Sabrun means to be patient.

Allah loves people who are patient.

Dhaad is for Dawun.

Dawun means light.

Light helps to grow crops and flowers.

ط - طـهـارة

Tah is for Taharath.

**Taharat means purity,
which is the Sunnah of
our Prophet Muhammad (SAW).**

Purity helps us to be healthy and avoid disease.

Zha is for Zolmatun.

Zolomatun means darkness.

Allah gives us darkness at night for us to sleep and rest.

ع - عِلْمٌ

Ayn is for Ilm.

Ilm means knowledge.

Ilm makes humans the best creation in the Universe.

Ghayn is for Ghaib.

Ghaib means that even without seeing, we have to believe.

We cannot see Allah (SWT), but we believe in Him.

ف - فَاتِحَةٌ

Faa is for Fatiha.

Fatiha is the first surah of the Al-Qur'an-ul Karim.

بِسْمِ اللهِ الرَّحْمٰنِ الرَّحِيْمِ

اَلْحَمْدُ لِلّٰهِ رَبِّ الْعٰلَمِيْنَ ﴿١﴾ الرَّحْمٰنِ الرَّحِيْمِ ﴿٢﴾

مٰلِكِ يَوْمِ الدِّيْنِ ﴿٣﴾ اِيَّاكَ نَعْبُدُ وَاِيَّاكَ نَسْتَعِيْنُ ﴿٤﴾

اِهْدِنَا الصِّرَاطَ الْمُسْتَقِيْمَ ﴿٥﴾ صِرَاطَ الَّذِيْنَ اَنْعَمْتَ عَلَيْهِمْ ﴿٦﴾

غَيْرِ الْمَغْضُوْبِ عَلَيْهِمْ وَلَا الضَّآلِّيْنَ ﴿٧﴾

Most Muslims memorize the surah Al-Fatiha and read it for prayer.

Qaaf is for Qur'an.

Qur'an is a revealed book from Allah (SWT).

Quran is the complete code of life for humans until Kiyamah.

Kaaf is for Kahf.

Kahf means cave.

Kahf hirah is where the Qur'an was revealed.

Laam is for Lahm.

Lahm means meat.

We eat cows', goats', and chickens' meat if it is slaughtered in Allah's name. It is halal and healthy meat.

م - مَسْجِدٌ

Meem is for Mosque.

**Mosque means
a house of Allah (SWT).**

**Many Muslim people pray five
times a day at a mosque.**

Noon is for Nass.

Nass means humankind.

**Humankind is the best creation
of Allah (SWT).**

Waaw is for Walye.

Walye means guardian.

**We strongly believe that Allah (SWT)
is our Walye, and we rely on Him.**

٥ - هِدَايَةٌ

Haa is for Hidayah.

Hidayah means guidance.

We ask Allah (SWT) to give us hidayah.

Hamza is for Adhan.

Adhan means a call to Allah (SWT).

We have to do adhan before we start every salah.

ی - يَوْمٌ

Yaa is for Yawmun.

Yawmun means the daytime.

**Allah (SWT) promotes the daytime
for good deeds and honest business.**

I love these books!
You may love them too!

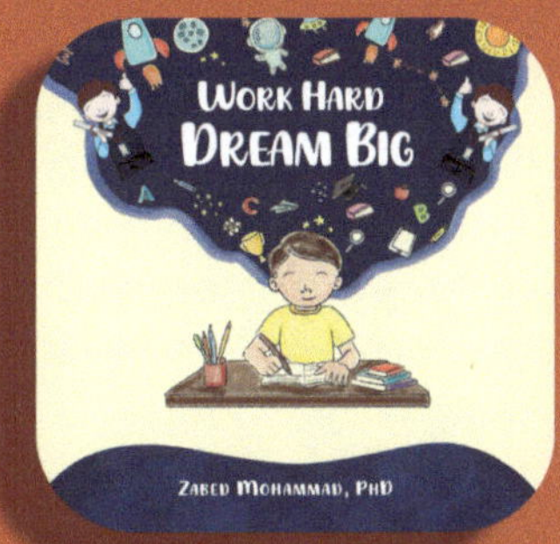

I am Zarir, and I am 11 years old. I live with my parents and two brothers. I wrote this book for my little brother to teach him the Arabic alphabet and his first few Arabic words. This book can be considered for little kids to teach them their first words or for voice/sound learning. For parents or elder brothers and sisters, by having this book, youngsters can learn the name of God and later on, they can discover a world full of learning. This book is designed to teach the Arabic letters Alif to Yaa, with Arabic words and more. Let us make the world a better place for learning.

info@kidseducare.ca

Copyright © 2023 by Kids Edu care Inc.,
All rights reserved
CANADA.

Library of Congress Cataloging-in-
Publication Data
ISBN: ISBN: 978-1-998923-10-6

Publisher: Kids Edu Care Inc.
Children's Dedicated Learning Series
Website: www.kidseducare.ca
Illustration Copyright © 2023 by
Kids Edu Care Inc.

Illustration & Design
Bee Digital